Going to W
in the
FIRST GARDEN CITY

A postcard issued by Airco Aerials possibly in the 1920's

The sidings and factories will be grouped together and screened from the residential quarter of the town by a hill and a belt of trees. In view of modern developments in gas and electrical power, steam is not likely to be largely used for manufacturing purposes, and smoke will be much less prevalent in Garden City than in larger towns. The establishment of manufacturing industries in the new town is an essential part of the scheme. The pressure of rates and rents and the congestion of traffic in London and other large centres are causing manufacturers to remove their works into smaller towns in country districts, and exceptional advantages and facilities are provided for these manufacturers in Garden City. Plenty of room can be allowed for extensions of the factory, and the workers are provided with healthy homes at low rents near their work.

From 'Garden City in the Making' August 1905
published by First Garden City Ltd.

Foreword

Letchworth, the First Garden City, was founded in 1903. The concept of the Garden City was to create, in the words of its founder Ebenezer Howard, "new towns to be carefully planned right away in the open country with a view to attracting industries from the overcrowded cities, and of providing homes for the people near to the scene of their daily work"

Letchworth was planned to have its industrial area separate from the residential area, but at its designed size of 30,000 inhabitants, no-one needed to live more than a couple of miles from their place of work, which was within walking or cycling distance. It is those places where most people of Letchworth worked that are the subject of this excellent and much needed book.

Some of the industrialists who brought the bigger companies to the Garden City not only provided their employees with a place to work but encouraged and provided facilities for their leisure activities. For example Dents built houses for their workers and Spirella provided baths, drying rooms, a library and a ballroom on their premises.

In the early days the First Garden City company put much effort into attracting industrial concerns to relocate in the Garden City with all levels of their workforce. As a result the buildings for the pioneering companies were in construction within two years of the official opening of the First Garden City site in October 1903.

Sadly the great range of products manufactured in Letchworth in its industrial heyday is much reduced. Many of the factory buildings pictured in the book, which we older residents still remember, are no longer there. Some are now adapted and used for other purposes, the Spirella Building being a magnificent example of what can be done.

Many people from surrounding towns and villages came to work in Letchworth. The poet Wilfrid Gibson who lived here between 1926-34 illustrated this in his poem:

JANUARY NIGHTFALL

A scintillating snake of jewelled light
Kindles the darkness as from forge and mill,
Free-wheeling gaily down the Letchworth hill,
The workers hurry home through early night.
Beneath the frosty stars, an endless stream,
One after one the little lamps shoot down
The long and gradual slope to Hitchin town
And happy voices call and faces gleam
Suddenly from the shadows, as they pass –
Lasses and lads released from bench and loom,
From clanging foundry and from rattling room
Where all day long beneath the roof of glass
On whirring wheels the live belts strain and scream –
Released at last, for a few hours to be
Masters of their own time, a brief while free
To call the tune and dance, or drowse and dream.

Allan Lupton, Chairman, Letchworth Garden City Society

The march for the 1926 General Strike came through Letchworth. They all stopped for a break at the Skittles Inn.

I would like to thank everyone who has helped by contributing postcards, ephemera and information. Without them this book would not exist. I think we would all agree that Letchworth has had a very varied and interesting industrial history throughout the last century and I hope this book will remind people of that. I know I haven't mentioned every company that has been in Letchworth, I apologise for that.

I would like to say a special thank you to Brian Waller and Don Brown for lending me some really good postcards.

Published by: Yesterdays World Publications
                4 The Crescent, Beeston, Sandy,
                Beds. SG19 1PQ
                Tel. 01767 699344
                www.yesterdaysworld@uk2.net
                Copyright Margaret Pierce 2015
                ISBN 978-0-9542771.4.0
                Printed by Adlard Print & Reprographics Ltd.,
                www.adlardprint.com

Cover: Workers walking past the Laker factory around 1910. Publisher unknown.
      Letter heading from Lloyds & Co. (Letchworth) Ltd., 1947

Relics of the "Good Old Days," Norton Village, Garden City.

The first industrial building to be put up in the Garden City was for the Garden City Press in 1905. Sites let or in course of erection in June 1905 were for Heatley-Gresham Eng. Co. Ltd., Vickers and Field and Ewart & Son Ltd. Other sites had been selected by Idris & Co. and the Garden City Laundry Co. Ltd. Several depots had also been established on the estate for the supply of builders materials etc.

Garden City Press Series.

POST CARD.

Communications to be Written Here. | The Address only to be Written Here.

Half-penny Stamp.

We have pleasure in sending herewith Cheque *for £ 80 . 1 . 11 to balance amount as per accompanying* Statement.

Receipt will oblige,
Yours faithfully,
GARDEN CITY PRESS LTD.,
Letchworth, Herts.

Two illustrations from the book about 'Ole Bill'

Book of the famous World War One character 'Old Bill' printed at the Garden City Press in 1916.

Employees of J.M. Dent visit Letchworth to look around on 18.5.06

Houses built for employees of Dents in Temple Gardens at the end of Green Lane. Postcard was sent to South Wales in August 1914.

Another view of Temple Gardens looking up Green Lane towards Norton.

One of the many street processions which were very popular in the early days of the Garden City. The cyclists are advertising Dents Everymans Library and following behind are Lacre Motor Lorries. They are passing the new station in the town.

Entrance in
Dunhams Lane
Published by
E. Housden

An early postcard of Dents premises, no publisher but possibly Clutterbucks.

The Aldine Press was built in 1906, one of the first factories to be established in the new Garden City. The range of books printed covered all kinds of literature – fiction, biography, history, travel, reference works and childrens books. They also produced 'Everyman's Library', the largest and cheapest collection of the classics.
This bookmark was issued by Phoenix Book Co. Ltd., part of Dents.

Lewis Falk, the Embroidery company started in Switzerland in 1888. Founder Max Herz was a friend of Ebenezer Howard who encouraged him to open a factory in the new Garden City. The factory was put up in Works Road in 1905 and the machines were imported from Switzerland along with male and female operators. Lewis Falk, nephew of Max Herz started in the firm as a boy and took over in 1936. In 1958 the company employed 250 people and made a variety of goods.

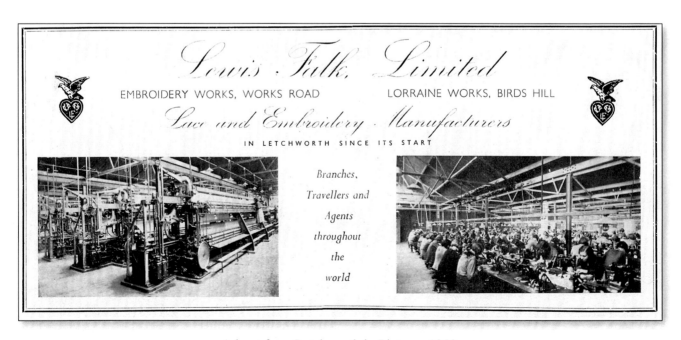

Advert from Letchworth in Pictures 1950

Advert from 1939 Letchworth in Pictures F.G.C Ltd.

Advert from 1950 Founded 1906 in Norton Way North

Drapery and accessories department, Letchworth, Hitchin and District Co-operative Society Ltd., undated.

Fancy dress prize winners in the 1910 Carnival of the Garden City Co-operators Ltd.

Both postcards were issued in July 1987 and the original photos are held by CRS Ltd,South Eastern Sector.

From 'Letchworth in Pictures' 1939 F.G.C. Ltd.

And you had to spend your hard-earned money somewhere!

Lloyd, Lawrence & Company was founded by John Post Lawrence in 1878 as an agency for the import and sale of America 'Pennsylvania' mowing machines in the City of London. In 1913 John Lawrence decided that Letchworth would be an ideal new location for the company. Over 100 years later they are still there.

Production of the first Letchworth-made Pennsylvania professional mowers started in 1934 and was followed by a range of other compatible equipment.

Customers of Lloyds include the Crown Estates, Royal Households and Chequers.

Many sporting venues are also customers – Cricket Test Match grounds, Open Championship gold courses, Queens Club for tennis and many other sports clubs.

A wartime advert

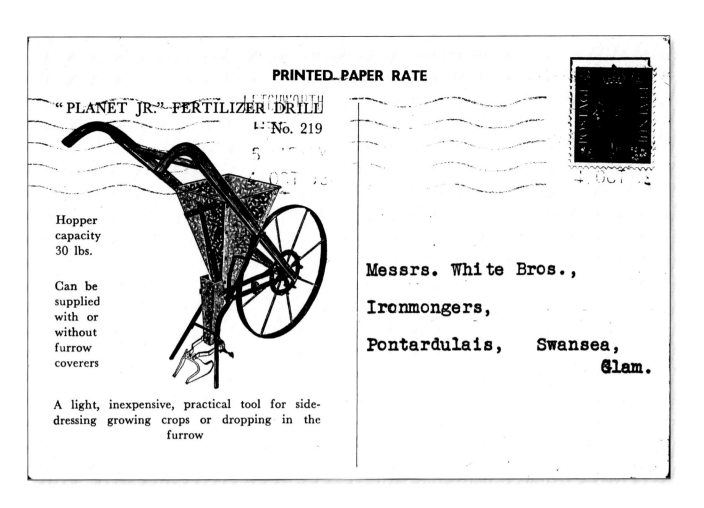

An advertising postcard sent in 1939 showing price rises due to the Second World War.

ALL COMMUNICATIONS TO BE ADDRESSED TO THE COMPANY AND NOT TO INDIVIDUALS

CABLES & TELEGRAMS:
PENNSYLVA,
LETCHWORTH.

TELEPHONE:
LETCHWORTH 139.

CODES USED:
A1. ABECEDARY, LIEBERS,
WESTERN UNION,
WESTERN UNION
FIVE LETTER

LLOYDS & CO. (LETCHWORTH) LTD.

AGRICULTURAL ENGINEERS,

LETCHWORTH.

PLEASE QUOTE REF:—

EF/JSL   Saturday, 11th October, 1930

Messrs. Abbott & Co. (Newark) Ltd.,
Newark Boiler Works,
NEWARK-ON-TRENT

RECEIVED
OCT 1930

Dear Sirs,

        We are obliged for your letter of the 10th
ref. GEA/NW and now enclose herewith formal order for
the five No.1 Handy Hoists with special cut gearing and
base of frame arranged to take four bolts.

        You will note that we are also ordering one
extra base of frame arranged to take four bolts which
is to replace that of the winch recently supplied.

        We are particularly anxious to have this extra
base as soon as possible and shall be glad to know the
earliest date you can deliver the same.

        Please say whether you can exchange it for
the base of the winch recently supplied which it will
replace, and at the same time advise us whether the
centres of the holes each side of the drum will be
6" apart.

                    We are,
                        Yours faithfully,

                    LLOYDS & CO. Letchworth LTD.

Ewart & Sons Ltd. was established in 1834 as sheet metal workers. Later they introduced and developed the instantaneous water heater which provided essential hot water services in the home. They were the first firm to acquire a site in the new Garden City and took three acres in 1903. The factory in Works Road was not erected until 1911 and in 1914 it was badly damaged by a fire.

The message on the postcard reads:

I've left Kosmos and am now an articled pupil to an architect, surveyor and estate agent (Edgar Simmonds)

Yours sincerely Fred

On the back is written 'Frank and his men at Ewarts Factory'

The factory in the 1920's

A postcard issued by Ewarts for the fallen and injured of W.W.1 who worked for the company.

When you specify

EWART INSTANTANEOUS GAS WATER HEATERS

you specify dependability

There are solid reasons for the dependability of Ewart water heaters. They are built to give long service with the minimum of maintenance.

✳ They have self-clearing steatite-tipped Bray burners that resist corrosion and blockage. The types of heat-exchanger employed are simple and designed to maintain a full flow of air and products of combustion, and thus obviate fouling of the flueways.

✳ Automatic gas governors are fitted to these Ewart water heaters to prevent over-gassing and ensure consistent performance, thereby prolonging the life of the heating bodies.

✳ Where pilot safety devices are fitted they are of exceptionally robust design. Alternatively, the interlocking tap safety device is of a well-tried pattern.

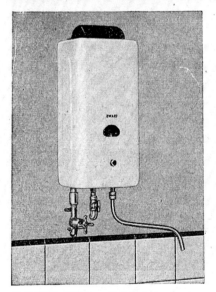 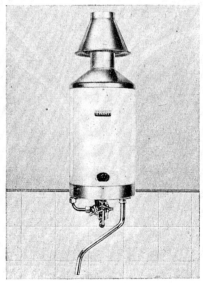 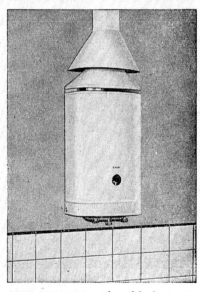

EWART M75. *A sink water heater. Can easily be adapted as a multipoint to supply two sinks or handbasins—through existing taps if desired.*

EWART S140. *A low-priced highly efficient instantaneous bath water heater. Will also supply adjacent handbasin through swivel spout.*

EWART M210. *A multipoint water heater which will supply instant and endless hot water in bathroom, kitchen, cloakroom, etc.*

 *famous for over 120 years !*

EWART AND SONS LTD • WORKS ROAD • LETCHWORTH • HERTS

CHOCOLATE CRUNCH.

Chocolate Crunch is Nature's Ideal CEREAL Food-Sweetmeat.

It is the Sweetmeat which all the public are looking and asking for.

As an ideal sustaining food for school children and adults it has no equal.
A bar of Chocolate Crunch is a meal in itself.

There is WEALTH of HEALTH in every Bar. In fact, it is a food the value of which cannot be over-estimated.

It is made from absolutely Pure Materials—

Puffed and Toasted Cereals—oven cooked.

Snow-white English Refined Sugar.

The BEST of PUREST Chocolate.

NO preservatives, chemicals or colourings of any kind are used.

Chocolate Crunch is made at the Garden Factory in the Garden City of Letchworth in Hertfordshire

Chocolate Crunch comes from the Home of Pure Foods.

Sold in 2d. and 3d. Bars.

Manufactured only by—

Cream-of-Cereals (1929) Limited, Oto Mills, LETCHWORTH, HERTS.

Not much is known about this firm except that it only existed in Letchworth for two years.

An early postcard of Smiths Bookbinding works postally used in 1911.

Premises of W.H. Smith situated on the corner of Pixmore Avenue and Works Road.

Smiths employees at work.

S 2056   INTERIOR OF W.H. SMITH & SON'S BINDING WORKS, LETCHWORTH.

A Clutterbuck published postcard of the factory.

Factory employees leaving W.H. Smiths Bookbinding Works on a postcard published by The Garden Cities and Town Planning Association.

FACTORY EMPLOYEES AT LETCHWORTH.

The shop of W. H. Smith & Sons in Leys Avenue, Letchworth in 1941.

INSTRUMENTS FOR MEASUREMENT AND CONTROL OF TEMPERATURES, COVERING THE ENTIRE RANGE ENCOUNTERED IN INDUSTRY OR RESEARCH, HAVE BEEN MANUFACTURED FOR THE PAST 40 YEARS UNDER IDEAL CONDITIONS IN THE FIRST GARDEN CITY BY

FOSTER INSTRUMENT COMPANY LIMITED

Telephone : Letchworth 984-5-6   Telegrams : Resilia, Letchworth

'Letchworth in Pictures' 1950

FOSTER INSTRUMENT COMPANY LIMITED

This is one of Letchworth's oldest industries and has been making precision Instruments for temperature measurement since 1910.

There are few industries or undertakings which are not potential customers for our Instruments, a fact which has helped to maintain a steady level of employment through the years.

The range of Instruments has been continually extended to cover the changing needs of industry, and this has meant varied and interesting work throughout the factory.

Newcomers are always welcome and will find a friendly atmosphere where initiative and craft skills can flourish.

HEAD OFFICE – Pixmore Avenue, Letchworth, Herts.
Also at Stotfold and Clacton-on-Sea.

Advert from Letchworth Garden City Official Guide 1967.

Architects at work in the drawing offices of Barry Parker (one of the chief architects of Letchworth Garden City) at 296 Norton Way South, Letchworth.

Published by Letchworth Garden City Heritage Foundation.

Ebenezer Howard with a Four Square Our City Banner made in Letchworth postcard also published by the Heritage Foundation.

When E.T. Morris invented the Marmet Baby Carriage he chose the first Garden City with its congenial surroundings as the ideal place to start manufacture. This was in 1912 and in the First World War production was limited because of a shortage of materials. In 1924 another site was opened in New York and in 1937 the premises in Letchworth were extended to supply the export market.

A miniature Marmet Baby Carriage was made for Queen Mary's dolls house and folding carriages were made for royalty. The firm also made nursery furniture.

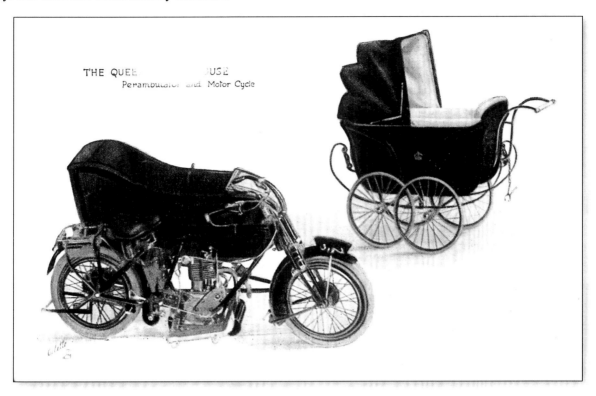

A postcard published by Raphael Tuck & Sons 'Among the miniature but marvellous articles in the Garage of the Queen's Dolls House, besides the Motor Cars and accessories are a Motor Cycle and a Perambulator emblazoned with the Royal Monogram, which will be the envy of all babies.'

From Official Guide 1951

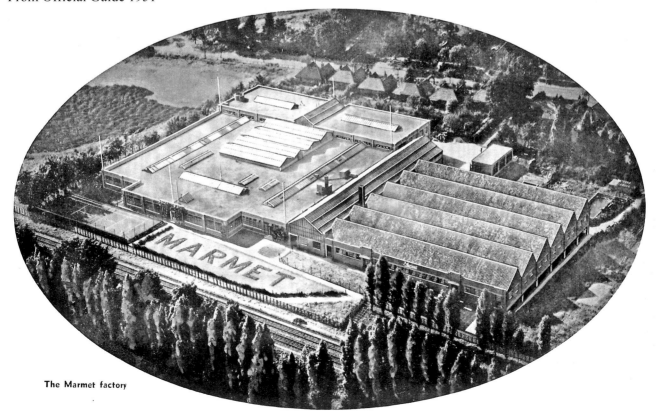

The Marmet factory

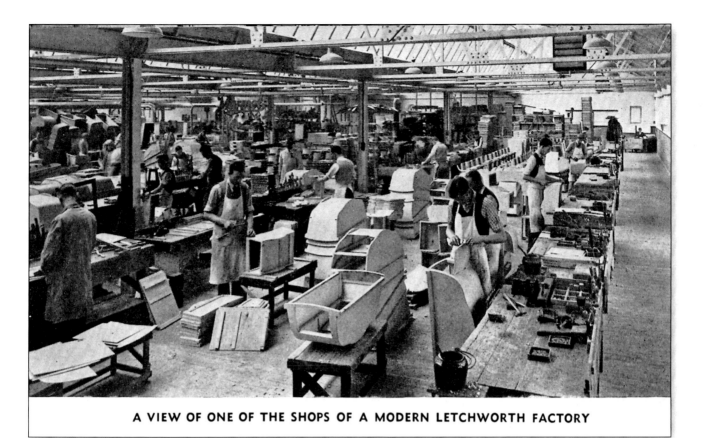

A VIEW OF ONE OF THE SHOPS OF A MODERN LETCHWORTH FACTORY

From 'Letchworth in Pictures' 1939

Colour illustrated: NAVY/NAVY

The Queen

A Baby carriage of luxury and Refinement

The spacious 43" superbly COACH-BUILT body has dipped arms, convex mouldings and triple fine lining. The luxurious interior trimmings include foam-filled cushions, and side panel with interior zip fastener pocket. The fabric hood, with exclusive Marmet pattern hood lace, and best quality heavily chromium plated easy lever joints, and the fabric over-end apron with additional storm flap, are individually tailored.

Nylon roller bearings support the strap hung body on a superior quality cee-spring chassis of tempered steel.

The tubular handle levers are oval and heavily chromium plated.

The wheels are 24" and 20" chromium plated ball-bearing, with a specially designed Marmet hand-brake de luxe.

Single colour only for the full beauty of its fine design.

Truly the Queen of baby carriages!

As an optional extra there is a folding pocket-end extension giving an extra bed length of 9".

26

Advertising leaflet from 1968

Postcard of the Lacre factory in Works Road, the message reads:
"This is a view of a model factory. This is the Motor factory which turns out the Lacre motor lorry. There are a lot of Lacre motor lorries in Capetown expecially on the South African Railways goods shed working.
It is very clean and is very pleasant to look at."

An excursion to Great Yarmouth for employees of Lacre Motor Car Co. Pictured at Letchworth Railway Station.

When Lacre moved into purpose-built premises in Letchworth in 1910. It had moved from Long Acre (where it got its name) in London. It built commercial vehicles. Harry Shelvoke became General Manager in 1911. J.S. Drewry was noted for his work on Pontoons for the Belgium Government and during their time at Lacre he and Harry Shelvoke worked on an easy drive and manoeuverable small lorry that was cheap to run.

Lacre was not interested and the two men left there to start their own business in October 1922. They had great success, moving on to refuse vehicles and special purpose vehicles.

The folder and photograph was issued by the company in 1953 to celebrate the Coronation.

Interior of 'S & D' Freighter Works, one of the machine shops.
From 'Letchworth in Pictures ' issued by First Garden City Ltd. 1939

The S.D. freighter
" W " Type 16/18 cubic yard Rear Ground Loading Fore and Aft Tipper

L.U.D.C Guide 1951

CONTRACTORS TO THE ADMIRALTY – WAR OFFICE – AIR MINISTRY – POST OFFICE.
CROWN AGENTS FOR THE COLONIES

· · · · DIRECTORS · · · ·
H. SHELVOKE, M.I.Mech. E., CHAIRMAN.
R. M. DAVENPORT, MAN. DIRECTOR.
C. R. FISHER, J. L. WILKINSON.
L. M. GOSTLING, M.M., A.M.I.Mech. E.

· · · TELEPHONE · · ·
· ·LETCHWORTH 234· ·
· · · ·TELEGRAMS· · · ·
SHELDRY LETCHWORTH
· ·CODE:- BENTLEYS' ·

SHELVOKE AND DREWRY LIMITED.

ENGINEERS.

LETCHWORTH, HERTS.

A. Fuller, Esq.,
81, Suffield Road,
Gorleston-on-Sea,
Nr. GT. YARMOUTH,
Norfolk.

FRIDAY,
2nd July
1 9 5 4.

Dear Sir,

Your letter of the 28th June in which you are seeking employment as a Storekeeper has been handed to me, but I regret there are no vacancies in these Works to suit you at the moment.

I have, however, recorded your address, and in the event of any alteration regarding the position will get in touch with you.

Yours faithfully,
SHELVOKE AND DREWRY LIMITED

F. Newland

FN/AA

Stores Superintendent.

...and in the end we chose  MEREDEW *furniture*

Firstly, the Meredew Book made our planning so easy

Sideboard No. 4802 £37.16.0

Veneered with Oak

*Cabinet No. 4304
£36.17.6*

Secondly, we found Meredew had the widest range

Veneered with French Walnut

and finally, it was so reasonably priced.

*Table No. 4007 £14.17.3
Chairs No. 4113 £4.10.3 each*

Veneered in Oak with Tola fronts

MEREDEW *furniture*

**Get your copy of the new 1956 Meredew
Furniture Book from your retailer or
send a postcard to:**

D. MEREDEW LIMITED · LETCHWORTH · HERTS

From Ideal Home April/May 1956

D. Meredew Ltd. came to Letchworth from the East End of London in 1914. Mr. Fred Hard, proprietor wanted to provide a better environment for his workers. The factory now employs 300 workers (1951). As well as bedroom and lounge furniture cabinets for the radio and television industry were being made in the 1950's.

Laundry and Kinora works pre 1914 in Pixmore Avenue,
it became North Herts Laundries in 1967

1939 Letchworth in Pictures

The Kinora company made photos and special viewers, I saw one at a auction once but could not afford to buy! The factory was destroyed by fire on 17th January 1914.

Clutterbuck postcards of the busy Garden City Fire Brigade

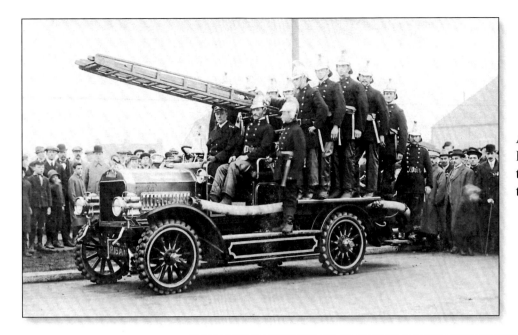

A postcard of the Letchworth Fire Brigade taking part in a parade in the town.

The Fire Brigade at work putting out a fire in Birds Hill.

A Fireman and his bride leave Church after their wedding 4th July 1914

HAYES REYNOLDS WORKS, LETCHWORTH.

HAYES REYNOLDS WORKS, LETCHWORTH.

Two postcards of Hayes Reynolds before the fire

4/5/13 Reverse of postcards reads: A photo of the fire yesterday at Hayes Reynolds Calico Printer burnt to the ground.

Postcard date 3/5/13

All postcards published
by Clutterbuck

All Clutterbuck published postcards of fire at Hayes Reynolds

Fred Notts bakery, Eastcheap c.1914 published by First Garden City Heritage Museum

On to different horsepower in the 1930's
Advertising sticker on back for Bennetts's Motor Works, Letchworth

Postcard published by Clutterbuck sent from Letchworth in 1920

Woodworkers Ltd. - Offices and Factory.

Message on the back of this CTL Series says 'Your Syd is amongst this lot meg. It was posted from Letchworth in November 1913.

Another CTL Series postcard captioned on reverse: Woodworkers Ltd., manufacturers to the trade of joinery, mouldings, furniture etc., Letchworth (Garden City), Herts. 34 miles from London (Kings Cross) Cheap Day Tickets 3/9 return, by train leaving Kings Cross at 11.10a.m. Half day tickets by train leaving Kings Cross at 1.45p.m. Sent September 1913

Woodworkers Ltd. - Interior of Machine Room.

Two Clutterbuck published postcards of Woodworkers Ltd. In Pixmore Avenue

A postcard of the Kryn & Lahy Steel Works sent to Belgium in 1928.

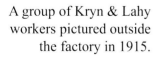

A Kingsway published postcard of Kryn & Lahy Metal Works showing the railway sidings many factories had.

A group of Kryn & Lahy workers pictured outside the factory in 1915.

A Garden City Steel Foundry.

STEEL foundries are not generally associated, in the mind of the average engineer, with garden cities and climbing roses, but rather with the depressing atmosphere of the Black Country. There are, nevertheless, at least three steel foundries of considerable size to the south of Sheffield, and two of them are surrounded by the most charming country, while as to the third, it is probably more the fault of the adjacent cement works, than of the foundry itself, that the atmosphere there is rather murky. The fact that one of the three is situated in Letchworth, the first garden city, is, however, to be accounted for more by the exigencies of the war than anything else, and we thus took advantage of the opportunity offered by a recent invitation to see how such an industry fitted in with the general well-being of a garden city.

It was, of course, hardly an appropriate time to pay such a visit, from some points of view, as the present labour dispute extends even into garden cities, and the normal complement of the works, of from 800 to 1000 men, has been reduced to only 100. We were told, however, that except in such abnormal circumstances the conditions of labour there are very stable, and that the men stop on in their employment indefinitely when once they have been engaged.

Reverting to the genesis of the works, during the war a large number of Belgian refugees was concentrated at Letchworth, and two wealthy members—Messrs. Kryn and Lahy—conceived the idea of putting up a factory with the object of employing that labour. Some land, amounting to about 27 acres, on the east side of Letchworth, and roughly a mile from the centre of the residential district, was consequently acquired, manufacture was started. Shortly after the Armistice almost all the Belgians were repatriated, and now the business is carried on under British management and the name of Kryn and Lahy Metal Works, Limited.

Taken from
'The Engineer'
9.6.22

FIG. 5—VIEW OF THE FOUNDRY FROM THE AIR

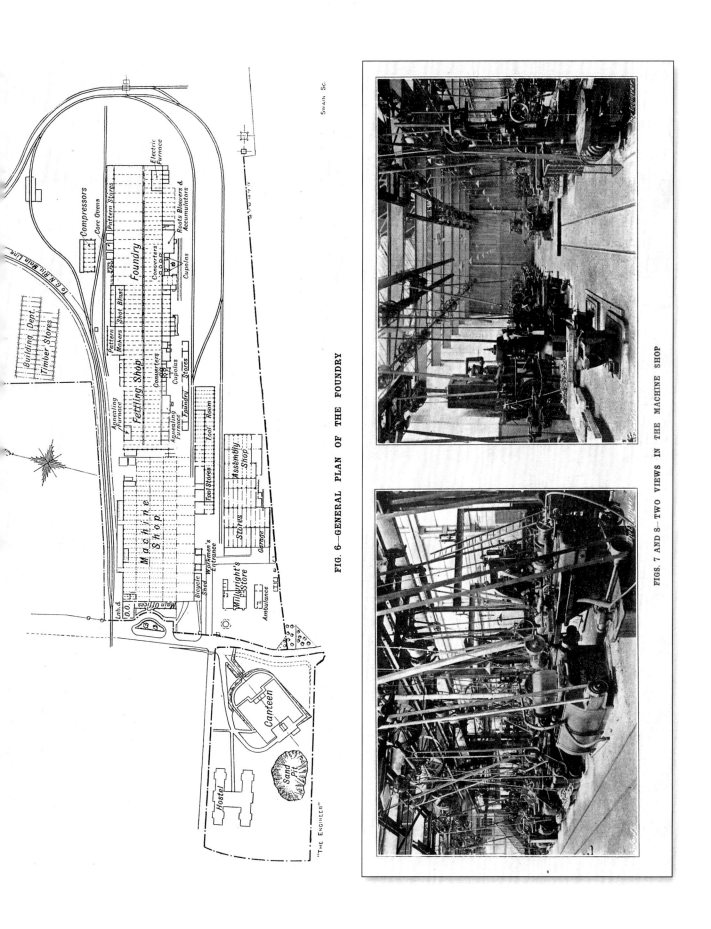

FIG. 6—GENERAL PLAN OF THE FOUNDRY

FIGS. 7 AND 8—TWO VIEWS IN THE MACHINE SHOP

From 'The Engineer' June 9th 1922

Made by the people of Letchworth

Designed to meet the exacting requirements of this modern industrial age—the products of both K & L Steelfounders and Browett Lindley uphold the finest traditions of British Engineering throughout the world.

JONES KL CRANES · STEEL CASTINGS · COBORN ANVILS · STEAM ENGINES COMPRESSORS · BROWETT COBORN PETROL/VO ENGINES.

FOR THE WORLD!

CRANES

The full range of Jones KL Mobile Cranes includes :—
The KL15—for loads up to 15 cwt.
The KL22—for loads up to 2 tons.
The KL44—for loads up to 4 tons.
The KL100—Rail Shunting Crane for loads up to 5 tons.

ANVILS

Specially treated to give deep tool steel face and hardened for long wearing properties.

STEEL CASTINGS

"Quality - Control" which extends over all K & L foundry processes ensures high grade steel castings.

PETROL/V.O. ENGINES

Air cooled, single cylinder, 4 stroke engines for operation on petrol/vaporising oil.

K & L STEELFOUNDERS AND ENGINEERS LTD

in association with

BROWETT LINDLEY LIMITED

K&L STEELFOUNDERS AND ENGINEERS LTD

L E T C H W O R T H ✳ H E R T S ✳ E N G L A N D

Telephone: Letchworth 2360   Telegrams: Kayell, Letchworth   Telex: 82112

Letchworth Garden City Official Guide 1967

A5

About Piano-Players
by an Organ-builder

THE internal mechanism of a piano-player is mysteriously intricate; and when it chances to go wrong, quite obviously its repair needs a very special class of trained ability. We believe you will be glad to know there are craftsmen working in your own town who are trained in the field of mechanics to which the piano-player action belongs.

¶ On the outside, one is not immediately aware of any similarity between the construction of a piano-player and that of a church organ; but, behind the surface, the likeness is most marked. In both, wind is the motive power; in both the piano-player and the modern organ, small pneumatic "motors" are the driving units, doing for the organ-builder what the steam-driven piston does for the locomotive engineer.

¶ Because of this we are specially fitted to give advice and assistance in any piano-player trouble, and we are glad to place at your service our skill in this direction. If you will come to us for this class of work we will endeavour to give you prompt satisfaction at a moderate cost.

¶ Even if you are not needing our services at this moment, it is likely that you will be interested in the work we do. The intricacies of organ-construction are interesting to most people, and if you are fond of work and workshops, or of music and musical crafts, you will be a welcome visitor to our workshop in Pixmore Way, at any time.

A. W. Hayter & Son
Garden City Organ Works
Pixmore Way
Letchworth

The Phoenix Car Company opened in Pixmore Avenue Letchworth in 1911 run by J. Van Hooydonk and A.F. Ilsley as joint managing directors. Albert Bowyer-Lowe joined the company as designer in 1906. During the First World War the factory was used to make munitions and after the war Bowyer-Lowe left the company. He disagreed with the management decision to only make large cars, he felt smaller cars were the future. The company continued to make cars until it closed in 1927.

On September 25th 1920 the Phoenix Paint shop went up in flames at 10p.m. This is shown on a postcard published by the photographer R.J. Salter.

Fourth National Spirella Training School held in 1914 in the Spirella ballroom

Sixth National Training School held in August 1916

A Spirella postcard from October 1961
The message reads: *I shall be in Deanshangar on Wednesday afternoon next, 1st November, and hope it will be convenient to come to you at about 2 to give you a fitting. I shall know its alright if I don't hear from you.*
June Adnett

The Class Room, where instruction in Corsetry and commercial subjects is given during working hours, free of all charge the object being todevelop and maintain efficiency among employees.

Section of one of the large work rooms. Here, as throughout the building, ample light, ventilation and sanitation are carefully provided for, and ensure cheerful, healthy, working conditions for employees.

A view of the Cutting Department. Skilled cutters are employed in this branch of the manufacture of Spirella Corsets, which are made to order and supplied only through Trained Corsetieres, to the individual requirements of clients.

Postcard sent 23.3.1924

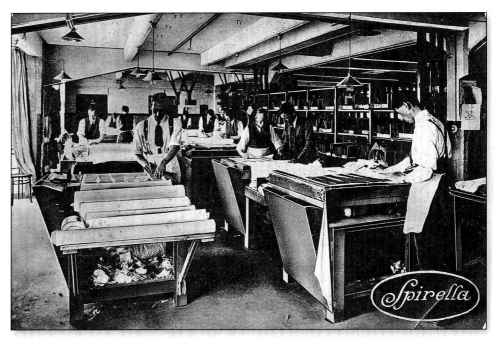

The Library at the Spirella Factory on a postcard by Clutterbuck.

Spirella
Fancy Dress Ball
April 12th 1913

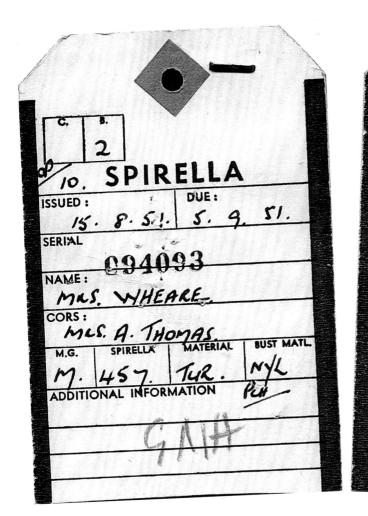

C.	B.		
	2		

10. **SPIRELLA**

ISSUED: 15. 8. 51. DUE: 5. 9. 51.

SERIAL

094093

NAME:
MRS. WHEARE

CORS:
MRS. A. THOMAS

M.G.	SPIRELLA	MATERIAL	BUST MATL.
M.	457.	TUR.	NYL PLH

ADDITIONAL INFORMATION

GNH

PLEASE KEEP   **THIS GUARANTEE**

Should a SPIRELLA STAY (illustration below) in this garment break or rust in ordinary wear within one year from date of purchase we will SUPPLY A NEW GARMENT OF EQUAL VALUE FREE OF CHARGE.

(Illustration of Spirella Stay)

Should the FRONT CLASP in this garment break in ordinary wear within six months from date of purchase we will replace with a NEW CLASP free of charge.

In the event of a claim arising under the guarantee, hand the garment with this tag to your Spirella Corsetiere.

NOTE :—Although this specific guarantee does not apply to CLOTH OR ELASTIC MATERIALS, Clients are assured that our Materials are the best of their kind and are thoroughly tested before use.

THE SPIRELLA CO., LTD. LETCHWORTH, HERTS.

Label for a corset 1951

Spirella surrounded by Letchworth views on a postcard published by Valentines and sent in 1952.

This postcard of 'The Factory in a garden' was sent in August 1931 with the message 'Just a postcard of the Famous Factory which I thought may interest you'

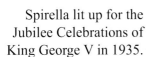

Spirella lit up for the Jubilee Celebrations of King George V in 1935.

Spirella came to Letchworth in 1910 and operated from the sheds in Nevills Road. The first section of the new premises across the road in Bridge Road were opened in 1913, the centre portion followed in 1917 and the building of the west wing followed in 1920.

The American founders of the company were forward-looking in their outlook from the beginning and sought a site for their factory where industrial welfare conditions were of the highest order, one of the reasons the First Garden City was chosen.

Originally the company came from Meadville, Pennsylvania and became an international organisation. The British public were served by a retail distribution service of 5,000 independent Spirella corsetieres with London premises at Spirella House, Oxford Circus, W.I. And in the early fifties opened a subsidiary factory in Harlow on the Herts-Essex border. They also had a stand every year at the Ideal Home Exhibition.

Owner William Kincaid made a generous donation to the settlement for a new extension. The company later came into British ownership and manufactured clothes as well as the original corsets.

Front and back covers to the C.G.A Catalogue for Spring 1921

[Photo by Sports and General Press Agency, Ltd

F54—W. H. SMITH & SON, THE ARDEN PRESS, STAMFORD STREET, LONDON, S.E.1

Workers at C.G.A all dressed up for a procession.

THE COUNTRY GENTLEMEN'S ASSOCIATION LTD

TELEPHONE:
LETCHWORTH 194 (4 LINES)

TELEGRAMS:
RURALNESS LETCHWORTH

CHAIRMAN OF DIRECTORS
LT.COL.WM.SELBY-LOWNDES,O.B.E.,LH.,T.D.

DIRECTORS:
J. H. A. WHITLEY, J.P.
LT.-COL. D.W. A. D. MACKENZIE, C.V.O., D.S.O.

CAPT. E.H.J.DUBERLY, M.C.) Managing Directors.
H.W.ACLAND TROYTE,M.C.J

HEAD OFFICE AND WORKS:

LETCHWORTH · HERTS.

IN REPLYING PLEASE QUOTE

E/1185/G   JB/MH

REGISTERED OFFICE:
LONDON.
CARLTON HOUSE, Lᴿ REGENT Sᵀ, S.W.1
TELEPHONE WHITEHALL 4052 (3 LINES)

BRANCHES:
GLASGOW: 149, WEST GEORGE STREET. C2
TELEPHONE NO. CENTRAL 2433/4
YORK: 84 & 86, WALMGATE
TELEPHONE NO. YORK 4172/3

AND JERSEY

C.G.A

19th December, 1939.

Dear Sir,

   We beg to acknowledge your letter of the 15th instant with regard to the offer for the TeLeS Motor Saw made through the Members' "Offers and Wants".

   We regret that we will be unable to carry out an inspection of this ourselves, and we have therefore been in touch with the manufacturers, The T.L. Smith Co. asking them if they would be able to arrange for this inspection to be made.

   As soon as we have their reply we will write you further.

                    Yours faithfully,
        for THE COUNTRY GENTLEMEN'S ASSOCIATION LTD.,

R. Dean, Esq.,
E & S. Estates.

Country Gentlemens Association in Icknield Way West, Letchworth Offices and Warehouse.

The CGA at a County Show

On the back of the postcard is written 'The CGA will provide facilities for your rest and refreshment together with experienced staff to answer all enquiries. At Royal Counties Show, Kingsclere, Hampshire 24-26 June 1965 Stand no. 178.

The first premises for Morse Chain in 1919 were in the premises that were used by Smiths Book Binding on the corner of Works Road and Pixmore Avenue. From Letchworth in Pictures 1950

The Morse Chain workers pose for a group photograph in 1928 published on a postcard by Latchmore of Hitchin.

Stan Hills and his mother pose outside their newly rented home after moving from London to work in Morse Chain in Letchworth.

Letchworth in Pictures 1950

The Morse Chain Company was founded in 1896 in Ithaca, New York, by the brothers E.F. and F.L Morse, who had been making bicycle chains since 1893. In 1903 a division operating as part of The Westinghouse Brake and Signal Company was established in London, moving to Letchworth in 1919. The Morse Chain Company, as it became known, became one of the longest established companies in Letchworth. In 1929 the company became part of Borg-Warner Corporation which supplied the growing number of motor vehicle manufacturers.

They moved to the purpose-built premises in Works Road in 1951. The company had become a major U.K. supplier of roller chain, leaf chain, sprockets, clutches torque limiters and couplings for the growing industrial power transmission market.

This photograph by Herts Pictorial shows staff including Les Hills and Arthur Neal with Management and Mrs. Dixon.

The founder of T.H. Dixon & Co. Ltd., set up his first workshop in his London garden in 1911 and moved to his factory in Letchworth in 1921. That first factory was in Works Road and in 1965 a second factory was opened in Blackhorses Road, with my father Les Hills as Superintendant in charge of the factory.

As engineers to the paper, film and foil converting industries Dixon supplied goods all over the world.

Our standard Pilot Coaters are shown on previous pages in this leaflet. This photograph of a special version of the Model 160 (known as the 160/36) emphasises the versatility of these machines. It shows a machine adapted to suit research in the photographic industry and is fitted with refrigerated air section and spiral dryer. Just one example of how a Dixon Pilot Coater can be arranged to suit special requirements.

Sur les pages précédentes, nous vous avons présenté nos modèles standard de machines d'enduction de laboratoire et pour production pilote. La photo ci-dessus est une version spéciale du modèle no. 160 connu sous le no. 160/36 et vous donne un exemple sur les possibilités illimitées de cette machine. Ce modèle est spécialement étudié pour satisfaire aux besoins de recherches poussées dans l'industrie photographique et est équipé d'une gaine de réfrigération et d'un séchoir à escargot. Ceci est un exemple pour montrer que la machine DIXON peut être utilisée pour des besions particuliers.

Unsere Standard-Laborstreichmaschinen wurden auf den vorhergehenden Seiten dieses Prospekts beschrieben. Dieses Foto von einer Spezialausführung des Modells Nr. 160 (genannt 160/36) betont die universalen Eigenschaften dieser Maschinen. Diese Maschine wurde den Anforderungen der Forschung auf dem Gebiet der Fotografie angepasst und ist mit einer luftgekühlten Kammer und einem Spiraltrockner ausgerüstet. Das soll nur ein Beispiel sein, um Ihnen zu zeigen, wie eine DIXON Laborstreichmaschine Sonderwünschen gerecht werden kann.

In questo opuscolo sono illustrate le nostre macchine standard da laboratorio e per impianti pilota di spalmatura, impregnazione, accoppiamento ecc. Questa fotografia, illustrante una versione particolare del modello 160 - conosciuto come modello 160/36 - dà rilievo alla versatilità di questa macchina. Essa mostra una macchina adatta alle ricerche dell'industria fotografica ed è attrezzata con una sezione ad aria refrigerata ed essiccatrice a spirale. Questo è solo un esempio di come le macchine DIXON possono rispondere ad ogni particolare esigenza.

Printed in England

THE SAXON PRESS LTD., STEVENAGE, HERTS, ENGLAND.

Picture from Letchworth in Pictures 1950

Irving Air Chute of Great Britain Ltd., came to Letchworth in 1926. Mr. Leslie Leroy Irvin, an American designed and made a parachute to be used from an aeroplane. To test it he made the first jump himself and convinced the American authorities of the advantages of parachutes for emergency use in aircraft. He signed his first contract with the British Government on the understanding that a production unit be set up in the U.K. Letchworth was chosen because it was near R.A.F Henlow where parachute testing was being carried out. He had only intended to stay for six months but he took a liking to Letchworth and stayed until 1946.

At the outbreak of the Second World War Irvin was the standard equipment of 67 different Air Forces throughout the world and parachutes were being manufactured in ten countries. The number of lives saved before the Second World War was over 4000 and during the war over 45000 members of the allied forces owed their lives to Irwin parachutes. Post war the company became Irvin Great Britain.

IRVIN GREAT BRITAIN LTD.

Jaguar Aircraft with IRVIN Brake Parachute streamed

CATERPILLAR CLUB

This unique and exclusive club was formed in 1922 by Leslie L. Irvin and its membership is limited to those people, no matter what nationality, race, creed or sex, whose lives have been saved in an emergency by an IRVIN parachute. The name 'Caterpillar' was chosen by Leslie Irvin himself in conjunction with Lieutenants Harris and Tyndall of the U.S.A.A.C., who were in fact the first two people to owe their lives to an IRVIN parachute. There were two reasons for the choice of the club's name; the silken threads from which parachutes of the time were woven were produced by the Caterpillar, and also the Caterpillar lets itself down to earth by a silken thread it has spun. These facts also gave the club its slogan 'Life depends on a silken thread'. Each Member, on being accepted into the club, is presented with a membership card, and also a gold pin in the shape of a Caterpillar on the back of which is engraved the name and rank of the member.

In the first year, there were just two members, Harris and Tyndall, mentioned above, but by the outbreak of the Second World War in 1939, the total member-ship was approximately 4000. The UK roll has now grown to a staggering 31,495. Obviously, a large proportion of this total represents Service personnel who have been forced to bale out over enemy territory only to become captured, and the stack of Prisoner of War Cards that arrived every day during the Second World War was between 100 and 150. An individual file for most members is maintained, and some of the contents on the back of these Prisoner of War Cards make interesting reading.

Typical examples are :

"Dear Sir, will you please enrol me as a Member of the Caterpillar Club. I baled out over Holland on August 15th from a blazing Kite and made a wizard landing".

"God bless you Brother Leslie on behalf of my wife and children, as yet unknown".

"Dear Leslie, I'd like to thank you for the sweetest moments in all my life, when my parachute opened and I realised I was not going to die. Your 'Chutes are so good I am going to name my son (when I have one) Irvin as it was due to one in particular that I am alive enough to woo, marry and get me a son".

Many now famous names appear on the Membership Lists such as Tom Campbell Black, Geoffrey De Havilland, John 'Cat Eye' Cunningham of Comet fame, Wing Commander Douglas Bader, and Jimmy Doolittle who has saved his life by an IRVIN parachute three times. The list goes on and on, and obviously it is not possible to mention all the names in this short space. However, below is just a few extracts from various books written on Caterpillar Club Members' escapes.

Colonel Charles Lindberg of transatlantic flight fame saved his life four times as a pilot in the U.S.A.A.C. Reserve he was involved in a mid-air collision. The first occasion was in March 1925 when He jumped again three months later when the aircraft he was flying became uncontrollable in a spin. In September 1926 he ran out of fuel in fog during a St Louis-Chicago mail flight, and abandoned his aircraft : seven weeks later in the same run he was caught in a snow storm at night and baled out - for the fourth time.

Ref : ("Into the Silk" - Ian Mackersey)

"John Cunningham famous as a successful night fighter pilot and Chief Test Pilot of the de Havilland Aircraft Company qualified for membership of the Caterpillar Club before the 1939-45 war. On April 11th 1939, Cunningham accompanied the late Geoffrey de Havilland during spinning trials of a Moth Minor. The Moth did not respond to recovery action and both men baled out over Wheathampstead, Herts".

(Ref: "Into the Silk" - Ian Mackersey)

"Ernest Udet, famous ace of the 1914-1918 war with 62 victories and who pioneered the 'Stuka' concept, became a member of the Caterpillar Club in 1934. Udet who was also famous for his exhibitions of stunt flying between the wars, acquired two Curtiss Hawk biplanes during a tour of the U.S.A. in 1933. Immediately on his return to Germany he used the Hawks to develop his vertical dive bombing concept. In July 1934 at Tempelhof Aerodrome, Berlin, the rear fuselage of the Hawk he was flying failed when pulling out of a dive. Violent flutter set in and, after a short while, the tailplane broke off. Udet survived, his parachute opening but a few feet above ground".

(Ref: "Luftwaffe War Diaries")

As you can readily imagine, we could fill many pages giving details of their exciting escapes, but we hope that the information given above just illustrate some idea of the concept of the Caterpillar Club and its many, many Members who are grateful to IRVIN's parachutes.

Caterpillar Pin (approximately four times full size)

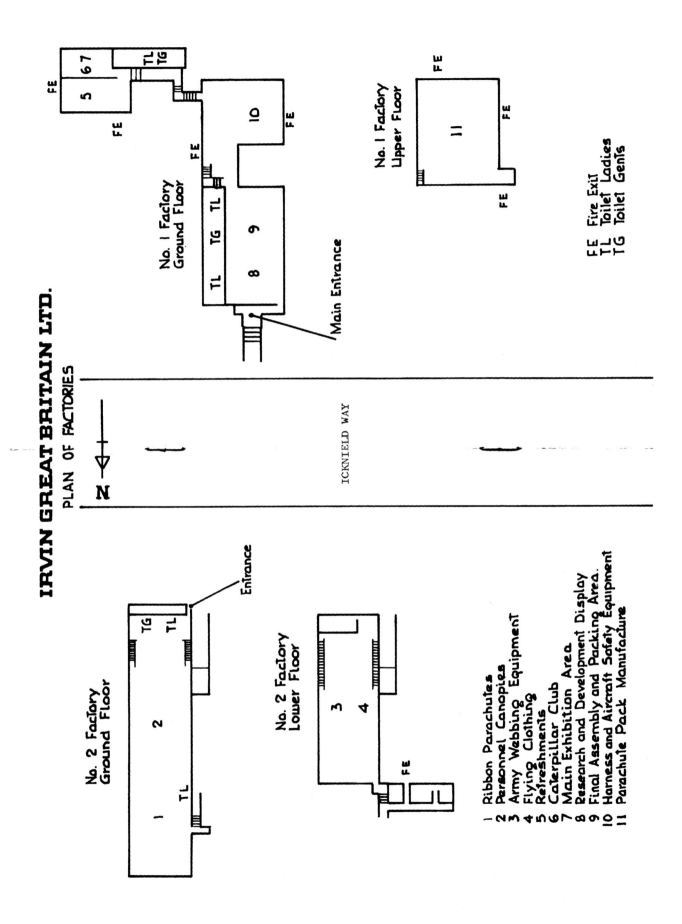

IRVIN GREAT BRITAIN LTD.

PLAN OF FACTORIES

N

ICKNIELD WAY

No. 1 Factory
Ground Floor

FE
5 67
TL TG
8 9
10
Main Entrance

No. 1 Factory
Upper Floor

11
FE

No. 2 Factory
Ground Floor

Entrance
TG TL
2
1
TL

No. 2 Factory
Lower Floor

3
4
FE

1 Ribbon Parachutes
2 Personnel Canopies
3 Army Webbing Equipment
4 Flying Clothing
5 Refreshments
6 Caterpillar Club
7 Main Exhibition Area
8 Research and Development Display
9 Final Assembly and Packing Area.
10 Harness and Aircraft Safety Equipment
11 Parachute Pack Manufacture

FE Fire Exit
TL Toilet Ladies
TG Toilet Gents

65

WORLD-WIDE CONFIDENCE

Since the War it has been the privilege of the manufacturers of Irvin Airchutes to supply parachutes of all types and for every purpose to Governments, Naval, Military and Air Forces, and Air Lines in the countries listed below. There could be no more striking demonstration of the world-wide confidence accorded to and instilled by the name IRVIN.

Argentine	India
Australia	Iraq
Belgium	Mexico
Brazil	Netherlands East Indies
Canada	Norway
Denmark	Peru
Ecuador	Poland
Egypt	Portugal
France	Spain
Great Britain	Sweden
Holland	U.S.A.

IRVIN

THE IRVING AIR CHUTE OF GREAT BRITAIN LIMITED
LETCHWORTH · HERTS · ENGLAND

Manufacturers of all types of parachutes for every purpose
Telephone No.: Letchworth 888
Telegraphic Address: Irvin. Letchworth

From The Aeroplane 26.8.49

The Letchworth Skillcentre's 50 years was celebrated in November 1980 by appearing on a First Day Cover.

The Skillcentre opened in what had been The Ascot Works in 1930. Prior to that it had been the factory for the Phoenix Car Company from 1911 – 1927. It was opened by the Ministry of Labour for use as a Training Centre for unemployed men from depressed areas of the north of England and South Wales.

As times changed many men and women from all over the world attended the centre to learn new skills and find a new start in life. It was said to be the oldest and most celebrated of sixty skillcentres operated by the Manpower Services Commission in Britain.

A postcard published by Larkfield Printing Company of the Letchworth Skillcentre. It shows the New Technology Section, Instructor Training College's, residential study/bedroom and Welding Department and probably dates from the Seventies.

Komos Photographics Ltd., of Pixmore Avenue were an old established firm in Letchworth since the early days. They manufactured a complete range of sensitized photographic papers for industrial, commercial and professional photographers, and they were big exporter around the world.

Advert from The British Journal Almanac 1954

In 1934 The Anglia Match Co. opened on a site next to the Abattoir. They made many different brands of matches including the ones shown here.

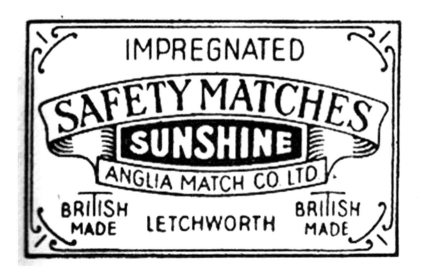

The factory closed down in 1954 after deaths in the management.

From Letchworth in Pictures 1939

Postcard issued by an unknown publisher of Sigma in the 1930's

The Sigma Instrument Company was founded in 1923 when owner Dr. F. G. Stewart began business in Stratford-on-Avon. The same year the company moved to Letchworth in Spring Road making instruments and equipment for the gas industry. After the death of Dr. Stewart in 1939 the firm began to develop fine measuring equipment which during the war became very popular. The company continued to make the range of gas instruments designed by its founder and developed high grade measuring equipment.

In the 1970's the firm was taken over by Alfred Herbert of Coventry and became Herbert Controls & Instruments Ltd.

Advert from Letchworth Garden City Official Guide 1967.

MISS D. GUNDY

SIGMA INSTRUMENT CO., LTD.

ANNUAL

DINNER

AND

DANCE

at

ICKNIELD HALLS, LETCHWORTH

on

SATURDAY, FEBRUARY 7th 1948

—PROGRAMME—

7.15 p.m. to 8.45 p.m. DINNER

A game of Whist is available in the Small Hall

9 p.m. Entertainment by Mr. Loss Pettengell

9.20 p.m. DANCING

Quick-Step

Veleta

Slow Fox Trot

Barn Dance (Progressive)

Waltz

St. Bernard's Waltz

Entertainment by Mr. Loss Pettengell

Paul Jones

Tango Rhumba

Old Fashioned Waltz

Quick Step (Excuse Me)

11.40 p.m. Last Waltz

THE KING

LAVINGTON PRESS, BALDOCK

Toast List.

The King

The Sigma

coupled with the names of Mr. H. Mc. Jack,
Miss A. M. Stewart, Mr. J. Loxham & Mr. C. E. Stuart
Proposed by Mr. G. Vernon

Reply for the Directors by the Chairman
Mr. H. Mc. Jack, B.Sc., M.I.E.E.

Welcome to the Visitors by
Mr. J. Loxham, M.I. Mech. E., M.I. Prod. E.

Reply for the Visitors by
Mr. G. C. Hibbert, Director and General Manager of
Messrs. E. H. Jones (Machine Tools) Ltd.

Menu.

Ox-tail Soup
Chicken

———

Peas
Roast Potatoes

———

Christmas Pudding
Rum Sauce

———

Coffee

A postcard from 1940 of the furnishing and removals firm John H. Green

An advert from 1939 – Letchworth in pictures published by First Garden City Ltd.

Improve Your Furniture With These Nico Fittings

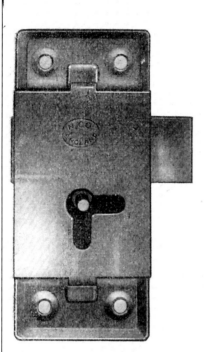

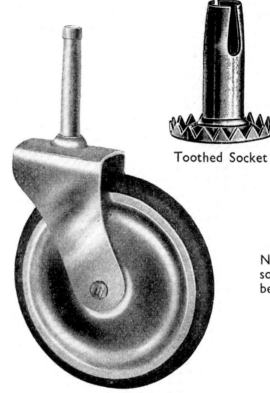

Toothed Socket

No. 1420. 1¼″ Castor with solid rubber wheel. Also being supplied with bakelite wheels.

No. 939. Lock with attractive one-piece flush-fitting case. Each lock being left or right hand.

No. 1309. Rubber-tyred Castor, complete with toothed steel socket.

No. 32
Straight screw stud

No. 33
Bracket stud

13/32″ threaded female brass catch — common to both 32 and 33

Note flush fitting

NICO MANUFACTURING CO., LTD.
LETCHWORTH, HERTS.
PHONE 590

Furnishing Trade Encylopedia 1950's

In the war this company made parts for the De Havilland Aircraft DH98 Mosquito.

TELEPHONE: LETCHWORTH 529.

TELEGRAMS:
NICOPUMP, LETCHWORTH.

NICHOLS COMPRESSORS, LTD.

MANUFACTURERS OF
Rotary Air Compressors and Exhausters

DIRECTORS:
S.H. BROWN *(CHAIRMAN)*
S.T. ANDERSON *(MAN. DIR.)*
W.W. BRABNER
R.J.J. HOPE-VERE

WORKS:
LACRE WORKS, LETCHWORTH
HERTS.

SOUTH AFRICA,
THE GRIFFIN ENGINEERING CO. LTD.
JOHANNESBURG.

YOUR REF.

OUR REF.

NL/MT

Messrs. Abbott & Co. (Newark), Ltd.,
Newark Boiler Works,
Newark-on-Trent.

26th February 1940.

RECEIV
27 FEB 1940
Answered

Dear Sirs,

Please quote your best price and delivery for the

following items:-

M.S. Support for Radiator.

1 off   R.H. to Drawing R.1155.

1 off   L.H. "   "   "

Your prompt attention would be much appreciated.

28 *Wo ea.*

74/- *ea.*

Yours faithfully,

for Nichols Compressors, Limited,

H Gray

Works Manager.

J. BROWETT LINDLEY (1931) LTD

ON ADMIRALTY, WAR OFFICE, COLONIAL AND ALL LISTS · TELEGRAMS & CABLES-SANDON-LETCHWORTH · TELEPHONE-LETCHWORTH 136 (5 LINES)

COMPRESSORS · STEAM ENGINES
GAS ENGINES · CONDENSERS

LETCHWORTH · HERTS

BL

OUR REF	YOUR REF	DATE
JA/MW.11815.		22nd January, 1940.

Messrs. Abbott & Company, Ltd.,
NEWARK-ON-TRENT...............

23 JAN 1940

Dear Sirs,   Plant for Ministry of Supply.

            We shall be glad to receive your lowest
price and earliest delivery for the following:-

            1, 4, 8, 12, 20, or 26 off- Vertical
            Mild Steel Rivetted Type Air Receivers
            2'-6" diameter x 6' high, suitable for
            a working pressure of 60 lbs. per sq.
            in., tested hydraulically to 125 lbs.
            per sq. inch before despatch.

            The Receivers to be built in accordance
with standard practice, and to comply with the requirements of the Factories Act.   Each Receiver to be
complete with Inlet and Outlet Pads, Manhole and cover,
Pressure Gauge, Safety Valve, and Drain Cock.

            Your price to include delivery free to these
Works, or equal.

            With your quotation, please give full detailed
specifications, etc.

                    Yours faithfully,
            J. BROWETT LINDLEY (1931) LTD.

For Elegance, Smoothness & Reliability

ESTATE *SLIDING* DOOR GEAR

An exclusive " snap-on " pelmet conceals all fittings and will harmonize with picture rail or panelled effect. ESTATE gear is approved by the L.C.C. and is stocked by hardware firms throughout the British Isles and in many countries overseas. Supplies are readily available from your local merchants.

For really pleasing appearance, maximum space economy, swift gliding action, and long life, always specify ESTATE Sliding Door Gear. Consider how easily a lounge can be enlarged to include an adjacent dining room. Again, how convenient it is to enclose a small area for heat and light economy or to provide immediate and intimate seclusion. There are many other advantages which will readily occur to planners who are interested in a high quality product at a keen competitive price. All such purposes are fully covered by the range of ESTATE Sliding Door Gear. Many housing estates throughout the country are using ESTATE Sliding Door Gear.

Please write for descriptive literature and erection data.

CLARKE ELLARD ENGINEERING CO. LTD.
WORKS RD., LETCHWORTH, HERTS. Tel.: 979

SEE OUR EXHIBITS AT THE BUILDING CENTRE, 9, CONDUIT STREET, LONDON, W.I
& THE SCOTTISH BUILDING CENTRE, 425-427, SAUCHIEHALL STREET, GLASGOW, C.2

GREETINGS FROM ELLARD & CHRIS BIGGINS

Reverse of postcard reads: 'Surprise, Surprise Chris Biggins Here – look, I've just had one of Ellard's super new doors fitted to my garage. It's easy to operate and looks terrific.

Why don't you get one? Ellards have 19 styles. For details on these super doors and other hope improvement products, fill in your name and address below and pop this card in a postbox – no stamp needed, Cheerio for now, Christopher Biggins.'

Mr. W. G. Ellard formed the company in 1946 as the Clark-Ellard Engineering Co. Ltd., producing light sliding gear for domestic purposes and mechanical handling equipment. In the 50's Clarke-Ellard concentrated on the manufacture of sliding door gears and the company changed its name to Ellard Sliding Door Gears Ltd. They were in Works Road, Letchworth next to Morse Chain.

ELLARD SLIDING DOOR GEARS
for all types of building and construction

The new ELLARD factory is continually being extended to facilitate increased production of the many well known types of ELLARD SLIDING DOOR GEARS. Increased production is absolutely essential to ensure that the supply of these products meets the ever increasing demand; and this applies especially to the manufacture of light metal garage doors which are extremely popular with motorists and site developers throughout the country.

The new premises provide excellent conditions for employees in both the factory and offices, where the work in all departments is varied and interesting.

Newcomers to the company are welcomed to a friendly, congenial atmosphere.

ELLARD SLIDING DOOR GEARS LTD.
Works Road, Letchworth, Herts.   Tel. Letchworth 2613 (5 lines)

Letchworth Garden City Official Guide 1967

WHAT DO YOU CARRY?

MEAT?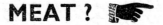

Hands Semi-trailer, Type NSSF, 8-10 tons, with lift-off insulated container.

Hands Semi-trailer, Type CJHS, 8 tons, with drop-sides and bolsters.

 METAL?

Hands Semi-trailer, Type CJHA, 8 tons, with 1,200 cu. ft. Pantechnicon Body.

MATTRESSES?

 MACHINERY?

Hands Semi-trailer, Type CSHM, 8-10 tons, with full drop frame and detachable rear axle.

Whatever your load, we can probably offer one of our many hundred standard trailers or semi-trailers to carry it. If we can't, we will design you a "special."

HANDS TRAILERS

MANUFACTURED EXCLUSIVELY BY:

HANDS (LETCHWORTH) LTD.

FACTORIES: LETCHWORTH, HERTS,

TELEPHONE   ENGLAND.   LETCHWORTH 600

The Commercial Motor 1949

The company was formed in 1927 and developed into Hands – England Drilling Ltd.

Advert from Letchworth Official Guide 1967

Kingswood Manufacturing Co. Ltd., was formed in 1934 by William Cater making brushes. In the post war years it was situated in Fenners Building in the Wynd. At that time it made circular lathe brushes used by dental technicians. It was taken on by John Stoddard in 1950 who had been Printing Manager at Letchworth Printers where local newspaper 'The Citizen' was produce. The company became Stoddard Manufacturing Co. and many new brush products were developed. They had a new factory built in Icknield Way and another was built on the site in 1960.

The company is still going strong and moved into new premises in 2011 in Blackhorse Road. The company is now run by Michael Stoddard and is the oldest family owned manufacturing business in The Garden City.

From Letchworth UDC Official Guide 1951

The Letchworth Bacon company was situated on the corner of Works Road and Green Lane. In the industrial area but not too far from agricultural and cattle breeding land. It was a very modern, well equipped abattoir which supplied bacon and fresh meat to the eastern counties. A well equipped factory produced processed meat such as pies, sausages and canned meats.

The abattoir was capable of handling 300 head of cattle, 400 sheep and over 3000 pigs a week.

The company extended it's activities into the field of medical and scientific research by opening a collecting centre for pituitary glands and adrenal glands used for the manufacture of cortisone or acth used for the relief of arthritis and rheumatism. Other glands were collected for laboratory purposes at Cambridge University and other research centres.

Letchworth Garden City Official Guide 1967

Samuel Jones came to Letchworth in 1946 as the manufacturing unit concerned with precision punching of paper products. It started in a small way as an experimental unit and went on to manufacture pre-punched self-adhesive labels, tacky label paper, tacky tape and gift tags etc.

All merchandise manufactured within the group was identified by its trade mark 'Butterfly Brand', a replica of The Camberwell Beauty butterfly, and associated with their Camberwell Mill and engineering works.

Letchworth car parts manufacturer Borg Warner's 'Car of the Future' displayed at the Letchworth Trade Fair 1978 celebrating 75 years of Letchworth.

A postcard from The Garden City Collection by The Heritage Foundation.

In August 1955 the foundation stone for a new factory in Jubilee Road was laid by R.S. Ingersoll, chairman of Borg Warner Ltd., It was Letchworth's most up-to-date factory and was built in thirteen months. It was the only factory in Europe which was devoted entirely to the manufacture of automatic transmissions and automatic overdrives for the motor industry.

In 1957 a new production line was started for the manufacture of one-way clutches which were in great demand in the aircraft industry for starter drives and helicopter rotor drives. They were also used for military vehicles, spin-dry washing machines and agricultural equipment.

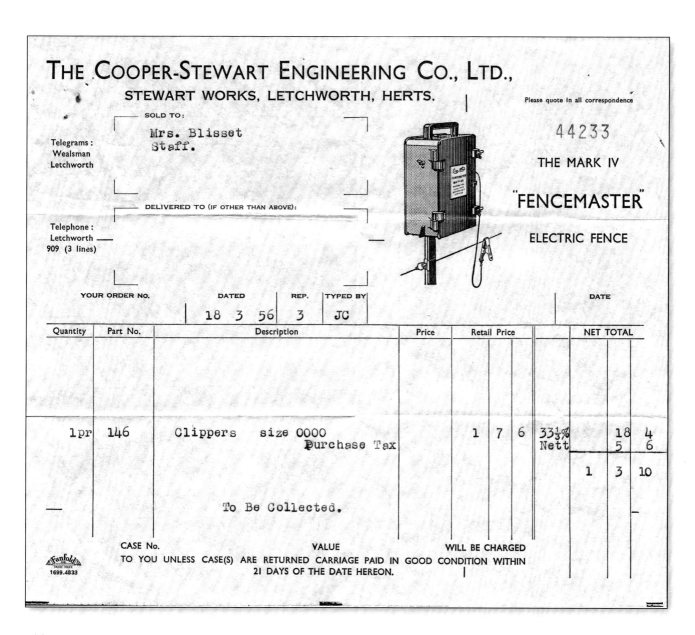

THE COOPER-STEWART ENGINEERING CO., LTD.,

STEWART WORKS, LETCHWORTH, HERTS.

Please quote in all correspondence

SOLD TO:

Mrs. Blisset
Staff.

Telegrams:
Wealsman
Letchworth

44233

THE MARK IV

"FENCEMASTER"

DELIVERED TO (IF OTHER THAN ABOVE):

Telephone:
Letchworth
909 (3 lines)

ELECTRIC FENCE

YOUR ORDER NO.	DATED	REP.	TYPED BY		DATE
	18 3 56	3	JC		

Quantity	Part No.	Description	Price		Retail Price		NET TOTAL		
1pr	146	Clippers size 0000	1	6	33⅓%		18	4	
		Purchase Tax			Nett		5	6	
							1	3	10
—		To Be Collected.					—		

CASE No.   VALUE   WILL BE CHARGED
TO YOU UNLESS CASE(S) ARE RETURNED CARRIAGE PAID IN GOOD CONDITION WITHIN
21 DAYS OF THE DATE HEREON.

Fanfold
TRADE MARK
1699.4833

This company later became Icknield Instruments Ltd., leading manufactures of speedometers, tachometers and gauges. It then became a part of Stewart-Warner Corporation, an American multi-national organisation.

The Works Road premises of the Hertfordshire Rubber Company grew from one bay to seven in twenty five years. The firm specialised in rubber extrusions, moulding, hoses and rubber bonding. Among it's customers were car manufacturers, companies making electrical goods and engineering companies.

In the war the company was exclusively engaged in government contracts. The company was also responsible for the development of the rubber components of the 'Comet' in connection with which commendation was received from the De Havilland Company.

From 'The Hertfordshire Countryside' 1960's

Tom Diss was a member of the Print Guild at St. Christophers School and purchased the Printing Shop there. With the Head H.L. Harris they began trading as St. Christophers Press in 1932.

They expanded the flourishing business and moved to the Tenement Factory in Works Road. Soon after they became a private limited company and moved again to Ridge Road in 1956.

When Tom Diss retired in 1968 the business was sold to Ladbrokes.

St Christopher
Press Ltd

RIDGE ROAD
LETCHWORTH

Letchworth 3737

*The standard of our garden has not
yet reached the standard and quality of our
printing — but we try!*

COME AND SEE ONE AND TRY THE OTHER

L.G.C Official Guide 1967

**ST CHRISTOPHER
PRESS LTD**

*Print More—
—Sell More*

**Works Road, Letchworth
Hertfordshire**

TELEPHONE - LETCHWORTH 609

Advert from 1939

Envelope from 1962

" Hollerith "
No. 1 Factory,
Letchworth

IN the eight factories of the BRITISH TABULATING MACHINE COMPANY LTD. nearly 4,000 people are engaged in the production of "Hollerith" punched card accounting machinery—the machine tool of modern management. The Company's No. 1 factory has been established at Icknield Way, Letchworth, since 1920.

At home and overseas, wherever the need for accurate, up-to-the-minute information arises—in Government departments, factories, mines and all forms of commercial activity—progressive management makes increasing use of "Hollerith" flexibility, speed and accuracy.

A " machine
tool of modern
management "

From L.U.D.C Official Guide 1951

5.30pm Cycling home from work at the British Tabulating Machine Co. and Shelvoke & Drewry's modern factories in Incknield Way. From Letchworth in Pictures FGG Ltd 1939

We like it here

It's always satisfying to be where there's an air of success. Especially when you're part of it.

After all, it's in Letchworth that we produce the 1900 Series of computers - a series that is enjoying unparalleled success both at home and abroad.

So that what goes on in Letchworth has, in fact, a great deal to do with I.C.T. being Britain's leading computer manufacturer.

 **International Computers and Tabulators Limited**
I.C.T. House, Broadway, Letchworth, Herts. Telephone: 5631

Letchworth Garden City Official Guide 1967

Inter-Works Sport League – One of the towns main sports organizations. Pictured here are the League's trophies, for which there is very keen competition each year.

Letchworth in Pictures 1950

Letchworth Inter-Works Sports League was formed in 1912 and, except for the years 1915-19, has carried on from strength to strength. Membership is confined to factories with offices in Letchworth. The League's activities include billiards, snooker, bowls, cricket, cycling, darts, footfall, hockey, netball, rifle shooting, running, swimming, table tennis, tennis and other field events. Rivalry between the different clubs is very keen and some exciting matches are fought out during the summer and winter months, providing good healthy sport for employees in the town.

The 'Chain Gang' at Morse Chain's annual dance at The Wilbury Hotel, Letchworth March 1968

Auto Club annual dinner-dance

SIXTY-FIVE members and guests attended our ninth annual dinner and dance, held at the Three Horseshoes, Norton, on January 16.

Following a lighthearted speech by the guest of honour, Norman Harrison, Tom Bremner, replying for the club, thanked Red Johnson and Norman Harrison for the cups which they have presented to the club. These will be known as "The Transmission Cup" and "The Morse Trophy," and will be rallied for each year.

Above : members of the B-W Auto Club at the dinner at the Three Horseshoes ;

In the late 1960's